Never Enough

poems by

Laura Gamache

Finishing Line Press
Georgetown, Kentucky

Never Enough

Copyright © 2017 by Laura Gamache
ISBN 978-1-63534-188-1 First Edition
All rights reserved under International and Pan-American Copyright Conventions. No part of this book may be reproduced in any manner whatsoever without written permission from the publisher, except in the case of brief quotations embodied in critical articles and reviews.

ACKNOWLEDGMENTS

"Carpe Diem," "Glove," "Before We Call the Bellevue Police Bomb Squad," and "Outing" appeared in *Sixfold Poetry Journal*.

Publisher: Leah Maines

Editor: Christen Kincaid

Cover Art: untitled painting by Charles E. Fulkerson, 4/7/1924—6/22/2014, father of the poet, from the poet's collection

Author Photo: Libby Lewis

Cover Design: Elizabeth Maines

Printed in the USA on acid-free paper.
Order online: www.finishinglinepress.com
also available on amazon.com

Author inquiries and mail orders:
Finishing Line Press
P. O. Box 1626
Georgetown, Kentucky 40324
U. S. A.

Table of Contents

The Unbearable Sadness of Bing Cherries the Color of Corked Red Wine 1
Behind Dad's Closed Closet Door 2
Carpe Diem 3
Never Enough 5
Five Lb. Coffee Can Full of Sand Dollars 6
Erase the Fears 7
Off Ledbetter Point 8
To Make This Easier 9
Glove 10
On My Walk to the Bank I Get a Call 11
Perfectly Fine Stuff Somebody Might Want 12
Before We Call the Bellevue Police Bomb Squad 13
Outing 14
Our Brother Who Art in Dad's House 15
I am Anxious About X 16
Letting Them Go 17
Real Estate Appraisal 18
Letter to Scott 19
Quieted 20
Día de los Muertos at Evergreen Washelli 21
Public Storage Unit B279 22

*The stunned drone of grief becomes the fierce,
tender undertone that bears up the world.*

—David Williams, from "Breath"

The Unbearable Sadness of Bing Cherries the Color of Corked Red Wine

> *With all best wishes for the success of your efforts*
> *in the cause of conservation. We welcome you*
> *to the great fraternity of those who have made treasure*
> *from what others have thrown away.*
> *-from Dictionary of Discards*

In Dad's workroom downstairs
where his paintings have been bashed
from their frames, punched in the face

our friend unearths the plastic faux Tiffany lamp
that hung over the dining table when I was fourteen,
ugly brass wall sconces from the 50's.

She says these pieces are retro and hot,
that our father's stacks of Road & Track
might be valuable.

I wish these gone:
spoiled jars of Bing cherries,
my parents' green dresser,
my great-great grandfather's
Knights Templar dress-up
in its moldering leather trunk.

Behind Dad's Closed Closet Door

Mom's and Dad's cremains hump
side-by-side in cheap laminate cubes,
Dad's in the creepy purple Neptune Society
tote bag the obsequious receptionist
pushed on me.

In a smaller cardboard box hand-cancelled
from a Yakima mortuary in 1984,
our youngest brother Mark's ashes.
Neat and tidy on the carpet
below Dad's moth-bit business suits.

Carpe Diem
> *for my sister, Lyn*

At my kitchen counter
with tablespoons and Sharpies,
we divided our parents' ashes
into labelled Ziploc bags.
I couldn't do that alone,
seeing those bits of bone.

I laid out my father's sand dollars
beside my Japanese ash-fired bowl.
They are smaller than I imagined.
Some are broken. Have I broken them?
I want more and bigger beach tender.
I want another chance.

Our parents are gone from the big rooms
of their enclosed lives,
their bitter squabbles,
their small and large sorrows and regrets.
Their shoes do not need them anymore.

Dad's Carpe Diem sweatshirt remains
on its hanger on his open bathroom door.
I drove his bathrobe through the tunnel
and down the chute into the finality
of the Children's Hospital donation bin.

No message echoes back
from the planet the dead flutter towards,
as they abandon us
to our pettiness and postcards,
the boxes neat beneath a rubble
of sticky dust and dread.

Do not ask for whom the wood curls
have been left across the work bench.
They are not mine, nor are the workings
of my brother's thoughts, the voices
above and either side of him that lead him
into the caves of their improbable conclusions.

Blood stains the indent where skin curls
to nail on my thumb. I tear at myself
in this quiet way to not cry out,

my mother no longer complaining,
my father not walking away from me down the hall.

Never Enough

Because paper bags are part-wedged, part-folded
beneath the bottom shelf that bulges
with what? in front of what?
and above that
Costco Danish cookie canisters
loaded with dead double A's
I cannot close Dad's pantry door.

The estate sale guy in jaunty beret
disturbs drawers, agitates laden closet hangers,
says there's not enough here
to make the sale worth his time,
hands me cash
for walrus tusk and thumb-sized mukluks
he pulled from mom's hope chest

she was always going to show me
some other time.
I'm the girl who freezes
as the jump rope whirls.
Our parents wouldn't "play favorites"
named the four of us joint executors.
I'm oldest, urged my siblings to opt out.

Five Lb. Coffee Can Full of Sand Dollars

Ocean tugs sand, hammers it flat again,
insistent as my sister on the phone.
I have vowed, but have not scattered
our youngest brother's ashes

along this verge where our mother
sulked near the invisible lighthouse
seeking agates and justification,

our father bent, a distant shape in mist,
to scoop another sand dollar
below smeared cliffs.

All three are dead,
and I still dread to do things wrong
and do things wrong.

Bell buoys gong
along this wretched coast.
I cannot hug their ghosts.

Erase the Fears

The realtor says that's our mantra
as he pretends not to be appalled
by the state of our father's house.

The downstairs ceiling sags with absent tiles,
Scott's survival generator hulks
outside the sliding doors,

rusty guts of an espresso cart
weigh down the wet bar, broken pottery kiln
dominates the garage floor.

I see a rat hole under the bird feeder
near the front steps. Scott shows me more.
I schedule exterminators.

He prunes camellia and rhododendron
to hairless arms, crops them below
windows, away from the house.

"Erase the fears," he repeats
when Lyn wants to strip wallpaper
she has always hated.

Off Ledbetter Point

A seal pops its human head
above the surface, looks shoreward
with large eyes,

dives to where sea stars disintegrate
to white goo. Hands grasping beach rocks,
there is nothing I can do.

Yesterday I dropped and skidded
along a filthy sidewalk. Scab on my forearm,
shoulder scrubbed pink as embarrassment.

I arrive home and remember
Dad's bloody wristwatch crammed in a paper bag
in my glove compartment.

On my writing table, Dad's wallet,
on the kitchen counter, his keys. Why
am I not that seal dropping back in the sea.

To Make This Easier
> *for my granddaughter Quinn*

Quinn is five, has drawn two girls.
Above one, she's printed "DED." The girl is dead,
Quinn says. The other is "DI," dying.

Quinn sits close, shows me pictures
of pirates that remind her of Grandpa Charlie.
I see how they do and say so. She scoots closer.

"My only regret," Quinn says,
"is I never got to draw
with Grandpa Charlie."

Glove

For handling dry ice; for glass cutting, sheet metal work, etc.
-from Dictionary of Discards

I try on a right-hand leather glove.
It is buttery and barely too big,
pull on the left, but can't. I'm confused.
Stare at it like a stubborn child.

The left glove has a thumb,
and three fingers, like my mother's dad,
who chopped off his pointer
with an axe, not careful enough
steadying wood on the stump.

He waggled that knob with the skin
stitched white-knuckle tight in our faces,
cautioned us cousins with his tale,
left behind this unwearable glove.

On My Walk to the Bank I Get a Call

The new representative for Dad's
car insurance company informs me
the other driver's "treatments
are ongoing." I say, "You do know
my father died in that accident."

I would rather not visualize
the woman getting chiropractic
adjustments and massages,
since what the hell it's free,
who broadsided Dad's Acura
with her Nissan Pathfinder SUV.

Pacing the sidewalk outside my bank,
I tell the rep to tell the company
to stop sending mail
addressed to my dead father.
I feel livid and helpless and too loud.

Perfectly Fine Stuff Somebody Might Want
Sewing Machine Needles: see Dentist's Drills
—from Dictionary of Discards

I box blocks of graph paper, most of it still white,
unused Christmas cards from Half Price Books,
card making kits for obsolete printers
that nonetheless sit on shelves,

wrapping paper,
factory curled bows,
Wit and Wisdom
for Birders, Quilters, Dummies,

fragile pattern paper pinned to fabric,
probably a collar, curled like a tongue
against the inside of a plastic storage bin,

my mother's late-life memoir class
homework, *don't read it,*
but I read: Unrealized Goals.

Before We Call the Bellevue Police Bomb Squad
"oh yeah, it's definitely live."
—Joint Base Lewis-McChord Bomb Unit

My sister pulls a white silk wad
from the box she seemed to conjure
from behind the shabby resin bench.
Under that his Marine Corps cap.

So this is where Dad kept the war
folded flat as a #10 envelope,
USMC buckle, inlaid boxes fallen
open, apart, handwriting on envelopes

that must have been his mother's.
These boxes must have been
his mother's. A wine-red watch box
with a fancy woman's watch inside.

Red sun Japanese flag with bullet hole,
yellow hand grenade, very small gun.
I reach my hand towards a book spine,
flinch from a second gun.

"Let's put this away," Lyn stuffs back
ripped shroud or parachute,
disintegrating boxes, letters from home.
Our brother John will want the guns.

Outing

> *Within these covers, you may*
> *find some use for your discard*
> *far removed from its original purpose.*
> *—from Dictionary of Discards*

Scott, Lyn and I station ourselves
in front of the bunker slits on the faces
of the recycling dumpsters in Houghton.

Steve from the Boeing Wine Club
already took two dozen wine bottle cases
but here we are with two carloads more.

"I'm Zeus," I say, after Dave Letterman
who flung fluorescent tubes
off a building roof in New York City.

I'm aiming for humorous, for light,
but the bottle misses and shatters.
Shards skitter across our feet.

Our Brother Who Art in Dad's House

thinks someone has come into Dad's house
to be sure Scott hasn't burned the place down.
He assures me he understands this.
I say, "but nobody's been in the house."

He has lined the deck perimeter
with thirty potted arbor vitae
so the neighbors can't see in.

He has taped a black plastic garbage bag
over the window in the laundry room door,
replaced the inside doorknob with a key-only lock.
I rattle it, but I can't get out.

I am Anxious About X

My friend says panic attacks
are brought on by imbalance, heredity,
but an anxiety attack stems from one stressor.
She says mine are anxiety attacks.

She says, say, "I am anxious about x
and that's okay." She says, "talk
to each body part in its own language."

Estates are businesses
and their lawyers charge fees.
We all pay for my questions.

My younger daughter says
it's like fingernails on a blackboard
when I gnaw the skin from my cuticles.

My brother wants to install
a security system at Dad's.
He needs to move out.

My sister talks about collecting
Dad's writing into a book.

My older daughter will
go into labor any day.

Letting Them Go
> BRIMSTONE: *see sulfur*
> —*from Dictionary of Discards*

I clutch timidity in jumbled shoeboxes,
fingers twined with tiny envelopes spilling
solitary buttons, Dad's Boeing 45 year pin,

my grandfather's name scrawled
in my grandfather's handwriting
on bank checks and on the frontispieces
of tedious outdated tomes.

Oh who would have these fraying afghans,
unflattering photographs in cheap frames?

I have known the poignancy of garbage bags,
and dumpsters, dumpsters, dumpsters.

Real Estate Appraisal

When I get to Dad's house
my brother is brushing his teeth
on the garage wheelchair ramp
our mother used precisely twice.

He shows me a tiny jar of ghee
and the health-club-huge treadmill
that dominates the dining room.
He bought both on eBay.

He's chopped camellia and rhodies
to bare branches below the eaves
like the realtor thought
would bring in more light.

I am here because he refused entry
to the real estate appraiser
I have begged to come back.
Pruned branches block the walk.

The appraiser has parked before
we've gotten anything tidied,
the yard waste bin prominent
in the street view photograph.

Letter to Scott

Leave this house of wounded ghosts,
our mother's avalanche of blame.

You cannot thrive here,

displaced tomorrows tidied flat
down the hallway of closet doors.

Rats chew beneath the bird feeders.
What we wanted is impossible.

Walk away.

Quieted

Mark's ashes have sat on Mom's sewing room closet floor for almost thirty years. Not long ago, Dad opened the door to show me. And Mom's, that have sat there for three. Too painful to deal with, Dad said. He didn't say he hadn't told their estate lawyer, hadn't taken her name off their accounts, or probated her estate. Brownie Ethel, Dad's Mom, lost her husband and her father in 1927, when Dad was three. All are now interred at Evergreen Washelli. Brownie Ethel had dealt with this, and two little kids. Lyn and I looked at their urns, shoulder to shoulder, squat and penny-colored, the first time we had met any of them. The columbarium director tells us once the niche owner dies that niche is inaccessible. "Quieted." Dad's sister, who died the year Mom did, had wanted her ashes interred with their parents'. Dad was not allowed to open the niche to grant Auntie Alice's wish, this woman who hardly asked for anything. We have just bought real estate: a niche as close as we can get to Brownie Ethel's. In the office of the columbarium, "largest in the west," we browse what seems, disconcertingly, the gift shop. The "view urn" looks like something you'd slather with mortar to build a wall: a dismal black block. I Google "Columbarium View Urns," order urn-shaped pewter ones. Mark had all the family genetic anomalies and new ones, died before he turned 21. His urn is engraved with a lamb, Mom's with a treble clef, she was a violinist. This is not the time, but Mom was also an alcoholic, Dad's sports a grape leaf, he made excellent wine.

Día de los Muertos at Evergreen Washelli

No *pan de muertos* nor marigolds at the Safeway
with Scandinavian flags, though I have found
packaged Day of the Dead skull cookies,
and my granddaughters Ruby and Quinn
carry tiny mason jars of water and salt for life.

I bring the estate checkbook to pay more fees,
try to duck briefly aside while my daughter parks,
but Lyn and I must sign more forms agreeing
to apportion ashes from our parents' cremains.

But this is festive, so we join the family
to pour water, salt, then flowers into the vase
we are directed to find in the staff break room,
fill another vase for Brownie Ethel next door,

troop across Aurora with the cemetery map
from Dad's desk, with its circled Fulkersons,
locate Dad's grandparents and Aunt Fairy Taylor.
Was she really a fairy? asks Quinn.

Public Storage Unit B279

What's left sits here in darkness
like dough that will not rise
in the damp, maybe decomposing
in this upright coffin off 405.

Microcosm of downstairs closets,
dim hidey-holes cleared and sold
or sent down chutes
to fatten other families' hordes.

I don't want to see these snapshots
in a retro-hip store, on an Etsy site,
don't want them,
any more than

long-gone Christening gowns sold
for $5 each, Mom's wedding dress
for twenty, the disintegrating crazy quilt,
or gramma's fox stole with tail and teeth.

It's cold here and I have to pee,
wedge back the protective tablecloth
furled around Dad's painted paper
and canvases I can't bear to toss,

refill plastic trays with DampRid, drive off.

Poet and teaching artist **Laura Gamache** earned an MFA in Creative Writing from the University of Washington in 1993, and directed the UW MFA Writers in the Schools program from 1993 to 2003. She was named a Jack Straw Writers Program fellow in 1999 and 2002. Finishing Line Press published her chapbook, *nothing to hold onto*, in 2005. Her poems and teaching essays have appeared in many print and on-line journals, including *Teachers & Writers Collaborative Press, Menacing Hedge, Sixfold Poetry Journal*, and others.

She works in classrooms through Seattle Arts and Lectures' Writers in the Schools Program, and was Sprague/Williamson Writer in Residence in Chiloquin, Oregon for nine weeks each fall during 2008, 2009 and 2010. She has written with and been inspired by students from five-years-old through elder adults. She walks, writes, reads and teaches in Seattle, where she lives with her husband, Jim.

www.ingramcontent.com/pod-product-compliance
Lightning Source LLC
LaVergne TN
LVHW041522070426
835507LV00012B/1754